IndraStra
papers

The Post-Pandemic World Order

Nine Pointers

Dr. Sitakanta Mishra

Faculty of International Relations, School of Liberal Studies
Pandit Deendayal Petroleum University, Gujarat, India

This page is intentionally left blank

The Post-Pandemic World Oder: *Nine Pointers*

This page is intentionally left blank

This page is intentionally left blank

About the Author:

Dr. Sitakanta Mishra is currently a faculty of International Relations at the School of Liberal Studies (SLS) of Pandit Deendayal Petroleum University (PDPU), Gandhinagar, Gujarat (India). Previously, he was a Research Fellow at the Centre for Air Power Studies (CAPS), New Delhi, and a Guest Faculty at the Nelson Mandela Centre for Peace and Conflict Resolution, Jamia Millia Islamia, New Delhi. He was also the Associate Editor of the *Indian Foreign Affairs Journal* published by the Association of Indian Diplomats, New Delhi, and currently the Managing Editor of *Liberal Studies* journal, PDPU, Gujarat.

Dr. Mishra received his Ph.D. from the Centre for South Asian Studies of Jawaharlal Nehru University (JNU), New Delhi in 2011. He was a Visiting Research Scholar at Cooperative Monitoring Centre, Sandia National Laboratories USA, during September–December 2013, and CRDF (USA) Visiting Scholar during April–August 2014. He is the South Asia Liaison of the International Network of Emerging Nuclear Specialists (INENS), London, and Visiting Research Fellow at CAPS, New Delhi.

Dr. Mishra has authored three books, one monograph, many chapters, and research papers related to India's neighborhood policy, Indo-Pak relations, India's foreign policy, nuclear policy, nuclear safety-security, terrorism, nuclear energy, cruise missiles, and South Asian affairs. He is also involved in Indo-Pak Track-II dialogue.

This page is intentionally left blank

Index

This page is intentionally left blank

Abstract

Will the world see ushering of new world order and arrival of a new global leader post COVID-19 pandemic? Such a systemic alteration to occur, some fracture in the ruling cohort is a pre-requisite. Has any irreparable fracture among the current global ruling elites emerged? Will the wrangling centered round the pandemic will prompt any fresh alignment and counter-alignment process culminating in a new polarity? Where does India fit in? Can India, while prioritizing domestic requirements, assume some global responsibility in an unfolding new world order to ensure a seat in the high table for itself? By connecting the socio-economic-strategic spats and crisis time power play in the wake of the pandemic this paper demarcates the broad pointers of the post-COVID-19 world order which may not be fully visible for next one year or two. If the US and European powers remain absent in shaping a global unity as usual, China and India may take the crisis as opportunity to start setting new rules and initiate actions according to their global governance visions.

The author suggests that a new world order is in the offing and with the strong leadership and global vision of Narendra Modi, India must look beyond the America-led world order, and both competing and cooperating with China, to usher the post-pandemic world order as 'Chindian world order' to its advantage.

Shut Your Eyes and Imagine…!

At the moment, the geopolitical implications of COVID-19 pandemic are undoubtedly secondary compared to the global health and safety concerns; but in long-run, the upshot of the pandemic would be consequential for the global order which at first has started to reshape and will fully transform to its new *avatar* at once. What would be the exact contours of the post-COVID-19 world order is too early to conclude; but given the unfolding power politics, especially between USA and China, and other actors like Russia, Iran and some European countries, the shape of current global power hierarchy would not hang on for long.

At the outset, the much expected cooperation between Washington and Beijing to control the pandemic has quickly swayed into a mutual acquisition which could be a catalyst for a future conflict between them. More importantly, in the wake of pandemic engulfing the entire world, a global power vacuum has emerged given the fact that all major powers consumed with internal problems have become inward looking for fighting the pandemic. All are aware of the fact that no nation is powerful enough to provide 'crisis leadership' globally at the moment. Does the absence of American leadership to deal the pandemic provide new opportunities for Moscow and Beijing? Will China maneuver for more aggressive international leadership as the United States falters; or the notion that 'China as world leader' just died given the massive negative impacts? Will America hatch a counter-strategy as it perceives Corona virus spread a Chinese conspiracy against its pursuit of 'Making America Great Again'?

Moreover, in this time of paucity of global leadership, will the world see arrival of a new super power leading the new world order? Can Modi's India, while prioritizing domestic requirements, assume some global responsibility in an unfolding new world order to ensure a high table for itself? Will the UNSC arrive at a consensus to recompose the high table by accommodating a new influential power like India which willfully shouldering the crisis-time leadership?

A systemic alteration of the global order to occur, some fracture among the current ruling cohort is a pre-requisite. Has any irreparable fracture among the current global ruling elites emerged? Will the wrangling centered round the pandemic prompt any fresh alignment and counter-alignment culminating in a new polarity? By connecting the socio-economic-strategic spats and crisis time power play in the wake of the pandemic and the consequent national and regional equations, one can certainly demarcate the broad pointers of the post COVID-19 world order – which the subsequent sections attempt to enquire.

Testing Time for the World Order in Vogue

In a way, the COVID-19 pandemic is testing the legitimacy of the global order in vogue and the crisis leadership ability of its chief protagonists. First, it is testing the agility of domestic governance of nation-states – the prime actors of international system; second, the relevance of global governance structures and institutions erected in the name of 'lasting global peace and development' in the post World War II period; and third, the ability and willingness of the existing 'super powers' to muster global response to a global crisis. So far, in all these respects, the current world order has faltered.

The propagated idea that the democratic governance is best to cater to the last man seems hollow today. The global governance structure based on liberal-capitalist framework nurtured by UN, IMF, World Bank, etc, has been a victim of power politics; nothing surprising today when China blocks UNSC discussion on the COVID-19 pandemic. More worrying is the shattering of the belief that a super power is one who is present every corner of the world and willing to control the global outcomes, if possible singularly or multilaterally. The COVID-19 has challenged this and has failed every known superpower of our time.

While America, the foremost superpower of the world, branded it "the Chinese virus," an American company has filed USD 20 trillion lawsuits against Chinese government for the creation and the release of the Corona virus as a bioweapon.1 On the other hand, China which plans to connect every part of the world through belt-road connectivity, seals its own borders to most foreigners to stop a second wave of virus spread. The interconnected world is locked down to stop the spread of the pandemic which many view as the beginning of the retreat of globalization or a reverse trend of global interdependence. Even prior to the COVID-19 pandemic, some countries in Europe, and USA, have chosen to disassociate from

---

1 Anwesha Madhukalya, "$20 trillion lawsuit against China! US group says coronavirus is bioweapon" https://www.businesstoday.in/current/world/usd-20-trillion-lawsuit-against-china-us-group-says-coronavirus-bioweapon/story/399071.html, 02 April 2020.

regional integration and insulate their border respectively mainly to prevent large scale migration.

In addition, the global governance structure centred round the UN and Bretton Woods system has been under serious stress today, and has been subject to manipulation during the last few decades by their champions itself. The recent example of obstruction of the UNSC meeting to discuss the pandemic-related issue, and the WHO position regarding China's dealing with the pandemic have renewed the longstanding debate about whether the world body is "sufficiently independent to allow it to fulfill its purpose." All these, and many more such instances in the past, give rise to a perception that the current global governance structure has become inept, therefore, warrant a complete overhaul.

Connecting the Spats and Faultlines

Before a full bloom, a new system in the offing normally amalgamates some deep rooted spats and faultlines to show the seeds of its arrival. It normally takes a while to build up to a precipitating stage and the outbreak of an event/crisis/war simply sparks its arrival. Apparently, during the last few decades, especially after 9/11, deep divisions are visible among the global governing elites over many global issues like nonproliferation, sovereignty, trade and interventions. The traditional alignments are fading and the international system seems to be moving towards a post-Western era. Gradually, the geostrategic pivot of the post-Cold War era has shifted from Europe to Asia and more specifically to Indo-Pacific. In addition, the world is pondering if China will replace America soon in the global power hierarchy.

One wonders if the COVID-19 pandemic is the alarm and the last nail in the outgoing world order's coffin.

The following nine visible symptoms would help visualize the broad contours of the post-pandemic world order. These symptoms, though not likely to superimpose at once, their gradual unfolding would herald soon the historic moment "when the world changes permanently, when the balance of political and economic power shifts decisively, and when, for most people, in most countries, life is never quite the same again."2

1. *Alternative World Order in the Making*:

Many would not differ that China is crafting a new world order through establishing alternative global governance structures and alliance systems. This not necessarily indicates the sudden demise of the America-led world order in vogue. What China seems to propound is a parallel global governance system "not to allow US monopoly to write the rules

---

2 Simon Tisdall, "Power, equality, nationalism: how the pandemic will reshape the world",
https://www.theguardian.com/world/2020/mar/28/power-equality-nationalism-how-the-pandemic-will-reshape-the-world, 28 Mar 2020.

of international order."3 The foundation of American world order in vogue is based on the Bretton Woods system, United Nations, and alliances crafted post-WWII, through which it could claim hegemony over redefining the rules of the international game. Certainly, China is a beneficiary of the "unilateral American military guarantee"4 and expanded liberal global order. But in the decades ahead it is likely to marginalize the US in many other spheres and with the ascendance as a major global player, it will strive to shape a world order of its own design by focusing mainly on three attributes.

China will further insulate its own backyard from external intervention and at the same time ensure other regions of the world not being dominated by any other power. Also, it will enhance its power to reach every corner of the world at any point of time; in other words, it will acquire necessary capabilities

---

3 Henry Kissinger, *World Order: Reflections on the Character of Nations and the Course of History*, London: Allen Lane, 2014, p. 362.
4 Ashley J. Tellis, Travis Tanner, and Jessica Keough, Strategic Asia 2011-12: Asia Responds to its Rising Powers, China and India, The National Bureau of Asian Research, 2012.

to become a stakeholder in issues arising in every part of the world. China has embarked on the 'strategic access' strategy by building artificial islands, seaports connectivity, and alliances. China has already set out to build multilateral institutions, like SCO, AIIB, BRICS, NDB, etc. by collaborating with like-minded countries, to provide alternative platforms for global governance and redefine the rules of the game.

Many observers consider the COVID-19 pandemic might reduce China's prospect to emerge as a superpower and undermine the leadership of the Chinese Communist Party. It was called China's 'Chernobyl moment';5 undoubtedly the pandemic has pulled China backward in its growth trajectory, but it claims victory in containing its spread using stringent mass quarantines, halt to travel, and complete shutdown of most daily life nationwide. "Beijing is working to turn these early signs of success into a larger narrative to broadcast to the rest

---

5 "COVID-19 really China's 'Chernobyl moment'?", https://news.cgtn.com/news/2020-03-07/COVID-19-really-China-s-Chernobyl-moment--OFecKsofew/index.html

of the world—one that makes China the essential player in a coming global recovery while airbrushing away its earlier mismanagement of the crisis."6 If China's claims to be believed, as the front runner in containing the pandemic, its "signature strength, efficiency and speed in this fight" has set "a new standard for the global efforts against the epidemic."7

At a time when no other global power could come forward to cater to Italy's urgent appeal for medical help, China publicly committed to sending ventilators, millions of masks, respirators, protective suits, and test kits. China has also dispatched medical teams and masks to Iran and sent supplies to Serbia, whose president dismissed European solidarity as "a fairy tale" and proclaimed that "the only country that

---

6 Kurt M. Campbell and Rush Doshi, "The Coronavirus Could Reshape Global Order",
https://www.foreignaffairs.com/articles/china/2020-03-18/coronavirus-could-reshape-global-order
7 Foreign Ministry Spokesperson Zhao Lijian's Regular Press Conference on March 5, 2020,
https://www.fmprc.gov.cn/mfa_eng/xwfw_665399/s2510_665401/t1752564.shtml

can help us is China."8 Citing its "comprehensive strategic partnership" with Iran, Beijing sent flights and medical teams to help the country which witnessed more than 1,500 deaths. Likewise, Beijing sent masks and medical teams to Italy, whose leaders have launched a "Hug the Chinese" public relations campaign, with disastrous consequences. President Xi has made a suggestion to his Italian counterpart on building a "health Silk Road."9 Alibaba co-founder Jack Ma has promised to send large quantities of testing kits and masks to the United States, as well as test kits and masks to many African countries.10

Beijing's edge vis-à-vis any other major power in material assistance is high for the fact that much of the material required to face the virus is made in

---

8 Campbell and Doshi,
https://www.foreignaffairs.com/articles/china/2020-03-18/coronavirus-could-reshape-global-order
9 Srikanth Kondapalli, "Coronavirus: Pandemic and power",
https://www.deccanherald.com/opinion/coronavirus-pandemic-and-power-818760.html, 28 March 2020.
10 Campbell and Doshi,
https://www.foreignaffairs.com/articles/china/2020-03-18/coronavirus-could-reshape-global-order, 18 March 2020.

China, be it surgical masks, testing kits or gloves; to meet the spiked demand in all these material China through wartime-like industrial mobilization has boosted these productions more than tenfold.11 China also produces roughly half of the N95 respirators critical for protecting health workers and produces vast majority of active pharmaceutical ingredients necessary to make antibiotics to deal with secondary infections from COVID-19.12 One commentary in China's state media threatened that if China withheld drug ingredients, it could plunge the United States into "the mighty sea of coronavirus."13

It's ironic, but because China was the first country to deal with coronavirus, it is now ahead of most of the world in terms of containment and recovery, therefore will reap the benefits from first-mover

11 Campbell and Doshi,
https://www.foreignaffairs.com/articles/china/2020-03-18/coronavirus-could-reshape-global-order

12 Ibid.
13 Louis Casiano, "Marsha Blackburn: China's threat to plunge US into 'mighty sea of coronavirus' means America must act",
https://www.foxnews.com/politics/marsha-blackburn-chinas-threat-to-plunge-us-into-mighty-sea-of-coronavirus-means-america-must-act, 19 March 2020.

status. Chinese workers are already returning to factories, while the United States and European economies are shutting down. When the world is clueless how to come out of the pandemic today, Beijing has a plan for tomorrow. "In COVID-19, Beijing sees the chance to win. This time, China benefits from a near-peer strategic position. It also benefits from first-mover status."14 Like it or not, China is maneuvering for international leadership by turning the crisis into an opportunity — to increase the trust and the dependence of all countries around the world of 'Made in China' especially when the United States falters.15

Therefore, the view that the "Chinese Communist Party has done more damage to China's prospects of

---

14 Emily de La Bruyere, Nithan Picarsic, *Viral Moment: China's Post-COVID Planning*, https://issuu.com/horizonadvisory/docs/horizon_advisory_ coronavirus_series_-_viral_moment?e=0%2F76651420, 15 March 2020, p. 5.

15 Josh Rogin, "How China is planning to use the coronavirus crisis to its advantage", https://www.washingtonpost.com/opinions/2020/03/16/ho w-china-is-planning-use-coronavirus-crisis-its-advantage/, 16 March 2020.

becoming a global superpower than its most ardent detractors" is shortsighted; and the notion of "China is fit to compete with America for global leadership is dead" is laughable.16 As per the *New York Times* report, "In sudden shift, US and China seek to cooperate as coronavirus pandemic rages on" and the US "administration is welcoming planeloads of medical equipment from China."17

2. *Towards a Xenophobic World*:

It is said that disease and prejudice go hand in hand. The unfolding post-pandemic world order will be coloured by some sort of racism or xenophobia (or Sinophobia) for some time. The mysterious Corona lethal disease seems exacerbating racism and hatred specifically in social media.18 The social media is

---

16 Jennifer Oriel, "The Chinese as world leaders? That notion just died", https://www.theaustralian.com.au/commentary/the-chinese-as-world-leaders-that-notion-just-died/news-story/bc64e3e82f20cb917705abcf86aba429, 02 March 2020.
17 Edward Wong, Ana Swanson, "In Sudden Shift, U.S. and China Seek to Cooperate", https://www.nytimes.com/2020/04/02/us/politics/coronavirus-trump-china.html, 02 April 2020.
18 "The coronavirus spreads racism against—and among—ethnic Chinese", https://www.economist.com/china/2020/02/17/the-

full of hatred for China and Chinese people. Conspiracy theories telling how China wants to kill others are circulating in informal social media. Reportedly in some places people with oriental or mongoloid features are now looked down upon as carriers of the pandemic. The "Chinese people in Asia and Asian people around the world have been treated with suspicion since the virus made international headlines."19 The Chinese diaspora around the world are being targets of racial slurs resulting from the fatal toll the COVID-19 is taking on humanity. Anti-Asian racism and xenophobia have continued unabated elsewhere as well. Singaporeans and Vietnamese are reported to be the targets of xenophobia and racism related to coronavirus in the U.K.20 Reportedly Canada's

---

coronavirus-spreads-racism-against-and-among-ethnic-chinese, 07 February 2020.

19 Eleanor Cummins, "The New Coronavirus Is Not An Excuse To Be Racist"
https://www.theverge.com/2020/2/4/21121358/coronavirus-racism-social-media-east-asian-chinese-xenophobia, 04 February 2020.

20 Suyin Haynes, "As Coronavirus Spreads, So Does Xenophobia and Anti-Asian Racism",

Chinese community faced racist abuse in wake of coronavirus; racist responses with Chinese diaspora communities have also been seen in Australia. "The coronavirus outbreak has taken a toll on Australia's Chinese community, including a loss of trade at Chinese restaurants and stores as well as increased reports of racism."21 In USA, and especially in New York City, mishandling of Asians has been reported.22 In India there are reported cases of abuse of people targeting mongoloid features in many parts of the country. People are being called 'Corona', physically abused and spat on with a clear intention of socially discarding them.23

---

https://time.com/5797836/coronavirus-racism-stereotypes-attacks/, 06 March 2020.

21 Jonathan Pearlman, "Australia's Chinese, Asian communities targets of racism", https://www.straitstimes.com/asia/australianz/australias-chinese-asian-communities-targets-of-racism, 10 February 2020.

22 Anna Russell, "The Rise of Coronavirus Hate Crimes", https://www.newyorker.com/news/letter-from-the-uk/the-rise-of-coronavirus-hate-crimes, 17 March 2020.

23 "Racism on the Rise against NE Indians amid Corona Pandemic Crisis",

Such sporadic incidents might be neutralized subsequently but for some time now onwards, the Chinese in Asia and Asians in the world especially with mongoloid features, will be subjected to additional health scrutiny or social seclusion while in transit.

3. *Authoritarianism Gaining Legitimacy*:

The post-COVID-19 world order will be marked by decline of democracy along with appreciation of authoritarian political system (read 'benevolent despotism') gaining legitimacy in the name of prompt implementation and containment of the pandemic. It is not difficult to prove now that "democracies being hampered by inherent inefficiency and political division" is proved ineffective to deal crisis situations in comparison to the authoritarian systems. "China's … success in coming to grips with the coronavirus pandemic as a strong case for authoritarian rule."24

---

https://insidene.com/2020/03/30/racism-on-the-rise-against-ne-indians-amid-corona-pandemic-crisis/, 30 March 2020.

24 Serge Schmemann, "The Virus Comes for Democracy",

The WHO called it "perhaps the most ambitious, agile and aggressive disease containment in history."25 As said by China's Foreign Minister Wang Yi, "only in China under the leadership of President Xi there can be such effective measures to put this sudden and fast-spreading epidemic under control."26

Meanwhile, in other parts of the world, according to a host of media editorials, "Dictators are using the coronavirus to strengthen their grip on power"27; "In

<hr>

https://www.nytimes.com/2020/04/02/opinion/coronavirus-democracy.html, 02 April 2020.
25 Lily Kuo, "How did China get to grips with its coronavirus outbreak?", https://www.theguardian.com/world/2020/mar/09/how-did-china-get-grips-with-coronavirus-outbreak, 09 March 2020.
26 Ministry of Foreign Affairs of People's Republic of China, "Transcript of State Councilor and Foreign Minister Wang Yi's Exclusive Interview with Reuters", https://www.fmprc.gov.cn/mfa_eng/zxxx_662805/t1745264.shtml, 15 February 2020.
27 Joshua Kurlantzick, "Dictators are using the coronavirus to strengthen their grip on power", https://www.washingtonpost.com/outlook/dictators-are-using-the-coronavirus-to-strengthen-their-grip-on-power/2020/04/02/c36582f8-748c-11ea-87da-77a8136c1a6d_story.html, 03 April 2020.

coronavirus pandemic, authoritarians around the world see opportunity to crack down";28 "Authoritarianism in the Time of the Coronavirus."29 On the other hand, all democratic governments in the world would draw lessons from the successful handling of the pandemic by authoritarian regimes like China and may inculcate a bit of benevolent despotism to their governance structures. This would be the beginning of gaining legitimacy for a new political system which can conveniently curtail civil liberty and democratic ideals in massive scale conveniently in the name of national emergency.

According to Florian Bieber, "Long before the virus hit, the world was already experiencing a decline of democracy. Since 2006, more countries have seen their democracies degrade than those that have

---

28 Guy Davies, "In coronavirus pandemic, authoritarians around the world see opportunity to crack down", https://abcnews.go.com/Health/coronavirus-pandemic-authoritarians-world-opportunity-crack/story?id=69795910, 01 April 2020.
29 Florian Bieber, "Authoritarianism in the Time of the Coronavirus", https://foreignpolicy.com/2020/03/30/authoritarianism-coronavirus-lockdown-pandemic-populism/, 30 March 2020.

improved. Last year, according to Freedom House, 64 countries became less democratic, and only 37 became more so."30 For that matter, the 'right-wing upsurge' is already visible in various democratic countries across the world, and "the pandemic will strengthen the state and reinforce nationalism" further; "Governments of all types will adopt emergency measures to manage the crisis, and many will be loath to relinquish these new powers when the crisis is over."31 "The trend towards centralised, authoritarian rule evident in countries such as India, Brazil and Turkey, and typified by China and Russia, has coincided with the rise of rightwing nationalist-populist governments and parties in Europe. Some are now following China's lead in attempting to weaponise the virus for political ends" opines Simon

---

30 Florian Bieber, "Authoritarianism in the Time of the Coronavirus",
https://foreignpolicy.com/2020/03/30/authoritarianism-coronavirus-lockdown-pandemic-populism/, 30 March 2020.

31 Stephen Walt, "A World Less Open, Prosperous, and Free", https://foreignpolicy.com/2020/03/20/world-order-after-coroanvirus-pandemic/, 20 March 2020.

Tisdall in the Guardian.32 In essence, the post COVID-19 order will nurture "a world that is less open, less prosperous and less free."33

4. *Cultural Superiority of the East*:

The post-pandemic world order will establish and propagate the cultural superiority of the East according to SD Muni: "The positive fallout of Covid-19 is that it underlines cultural superiority of the East over the West by replacing hand shake with Namaste. It is also underlines the virtues of vegetarianism over wild and bizarre eating preferences."34 Undoubtedly critics would point that COVID-19 is originated from the East itself; vegetarianism is practiced only by a minority of people in the East, and the Eastern culture is full of

---

32 Simon Tisdall, "Power, equality, nationalism: how the pandemic will reshape the world", https://www.theguardian.com/world/2020/mar/28/power-equality-nationalism-how-the-pandemic-will-reshape-the-world, 28 March 2020.
33 Stephen Walt, "A World Less Open, Prosperous, and Free", https://foreignpolicy.com/2020/03/20/world-order-after-coroanvirus-pandemic/, 20 March 2020.
34 SD Muni, https://twitter.com/SDMUNI/status/1238687810883747841, 14 March 2020.

superstitions, so on and so forth. But nobody would disagree that for long the Eastern lifestyle, habits, and practices were considered inferior to the Western practices; even the East emulated Western lifestyle madly in the name of modernity. Even if the entire Eastern cultural practices cannot be appreciated, many Indian lifestyle and cultural prescriptions for healthy life need to be praised. The Indian practices like Yoga, Ayurveda, Diya, etc. are likely to get wider acceptance in the world. This is not to discount or sideline other novel cultural practices in other parts of East or West. The Eastern values that were viewed blatantly inferior vis-à-vis the West will no longer withstand.

Similarly, as Stephen Walt views, the pandemic response discourse "will also accelerate the shift in power and influence from West to East. The response in Europe and America has been slow and haphazard by comparison [with China, South Korea and Singapore], further tarnishing the aura of the western 'brand'...."35 The traditional balance of power

---

35 Stephen Walt, "A World Less Open, Prosperous, and Free", https://foreignpolicy.com/2020/03/20/world-order-after-coroanvirus-pandemic/, 20 March 2020.

centred round Anglo-American narrative bound to shift to the East soon as both Europe and America would face severe economic crisis.

Undoubtedly the economic impact of the pandemic is global and will be felt in every corner, but the inherent resilience of the Eastern economies and lifestyle will help the Eastern people to withstand the crisis at ease than the West. Post-pandemic economic recovery of the East would be quicker that the West: given their market size and state protection, the Eastern economies would fare better in the subsequent decades. For China, "the virus has become a soft power tool to overtake its superpower rival, the US."36 China is reinforcing its credentials as a global leader by offering assistance to all badly affected countries. India also seems to seize the opportunity to extend some leadership in the South Asian region as well as leading the G-20 to shape a concerted global pandemic response. *If the US and European powers remain absent in shaping a global*

36 Tisdall,
https://www.theguardian.com/world/2020/mar/28/power-equality-nationalism-how-the-pandemic-will-reshape-the-world, 28 March 2020.

unity as usual, China and India may take the crisis as opportunity to start setting new rules and initiate actions according to their global governance visions.

5. *Retreat of Hyper-Globalization*:

The post COVID-19 world will be a re-globalized world with a "retreat from this phase of hyper-globalisation, as citizens look to national governments to protect them and as states and firms seek to reduce future vulnerabilities."37 On the one hand, the world may see "increased post-pandemic protectionism if, as some predict, countries attempt to limit future exposure to global threats."38 The economic globalization that the world has embarked on long ago would continue for some time as economic dependency through the Bretton Woods system has strongly been entrenched. But physical mobility of men and groups has already experienced a stiff decline which is likely to continue and physical

37 Walt, https://foreignpolicy.com/2020/03/20/world-order-after-coroanvirus-pandemic/, 20 March 2020.
38 Tisdall, https://www.theguardian.com/world/2020/mar/28/power-equality-nationalism-how-the-pandemic-will-reshape-the-world, 28 March 2020.

world will remain disconnected physically for a long period to come.

Simultaneously, there would be re-globalization of the world, or Globalisation 2.0, as Robert Kaplan names it, which will be marked by emergence of "great-power blocs with their own burgeoning militaries and separate supply chains, about the rise of autocracies, and about social and class divides that have engendered nativism and populism, coupled with middle-class angst in Western democracies. In sum, it is a story about new and re-emerging global divisions".39 Robert Kaplan sees "the coronavirus pandemic is an economic and geopolitical shock", "the historical marker between the first phase of globalisation and the second …. In sum, it is a story about new and re-emerging global divisions."40 The trade practices and supply chain system of the globalization process in vogue will continue for a while gradually giving way for the new parameters of

---

39 Walt, https://foreignpolicy.com/2020/03/20/world-order-after-coroanvirus-pandemic/, 20 March 2020.
40 Robert D. Kaplan, "Globalization We Were Afraid Of", https://www.bloomberg.com/opinion/articles/2020-03-20/coronavirus-ushers-in-the-globalization-we-were-afraid-of?srnd=opinion, 20 March 2020.

the Globalization 2.0 to entrench. The beginning of the end of the first phase of globalization and onset of the second phase has already been in progress for some time now. When the Globalization 2.0 will fully engulf the world is a matter of conjecture, but the globalized world of this epoch will not persist for long for sure.

6. *Towards a Virtual Civilization*:

The post COVID-19 world will nurture a "virtual civilization"41 as physical mobility of people will be significantly curtailed often during the foreseeable future. Given the worsening condition of the climate and repeated disasters will compel human civilization to restrict their mobility. Climate induced displacement is a fact but nation would be reluctant to support and facilitate migration anymore. It has been seen how many European and West Asian countries pushed back the migrants in the recent past. As far as control of the pandemic is concerned, the only effective method is social distancing and

---

41 Manish Tiwari, "The post COVID-19 world", https://www.orfonline.org/expert-speak/the-post-covid-19-world-63829/, 29 March 2020.

restriction of movement. During such a situation, connectivity through virtual platforms or the cyber domain is the only channel which has exponentially grown and sustaining the globalized world in its current nomenclature.

As the physical world has come to a halt and this would persist for some years, the cyber world will experience a corresponding overdrive. More innovation in virtual technology in decades to come would nurture a "virtual civilization" to flourish in the decades ahead. While social or physical distancing will be the 'new normal' or *nom de guerre*, virtual cohesion and capability will shape and drive the global discourse now on. But the world is likely to confront a new dilemma of how to make the virtual the real, as it is prone to intense manipulation.

7. *Crisis-Generated Alliances*:

The post-pandemic world will see shifting or formation of alliances on the basis of crisis time assistance, and floating conspiracy theories involving the source of, and intention behind, the outbreak of COVID-19. The conspiracy theories over the virus are likely to worsen China-USA rift in future while pandemic time sympathy and collaboration will prompt strange alliance formations elsewhere.

The Chinese version of the conspiracy theory, which Chinese social media abounds with conjecture, that the virus was engineered by the United States as an agent of biological warfare against China. A widely shared conspiracy theory says that American soldiers participating in the 2019 Military World Games in Wuhan deliberately shed the virus at the Seafood Market. On the other hand, the American version, accusing China of testing of biological weapons in its lab that got out of control, named it as the 'Chinese virus' or the 'Wuhan virus', and demanded accountability from China. The split between the two super powers is now wide open; which way it would escalate is a matter of introspection.

Meanwhile, global interdependence and the collective approach to address global problems that the America-led world order bloviated seem impractical. As America itself struggling within and unable to lead in this time of global crisis, the unconditional backup America used to enjoy from its European allies or NATO partners before would not be available spontaneously now. China on the other hand reached out to the worst-affected countries in Europe enthusiastically, signaling its strength to provide crisis-time leadership to the world. In other parts of the world, strange crisis-time partnership is evolving. For example, countries hitherto at odds such as Iran and the UAE are cooperating, at least temporarily. UAE has sent twice medical aid to Iran as coronavirus outbreak intensifies[42] even though it conducted a major military exercise with USA on 23rd March in the desert 125 miles southwest of Abu Dhabi.[43] In Philippines, the pandemic crisis prompted a ceasefire with the Communist rebels.

Pandemics are on the rise but the world's strategy for dealing with pandemics is woefully inadequate at the

---

42 "UAE sends medical aid to Iran as coronavirus outbreak intensifies", https://www.al-monitor.com/pulse/originals/2020/03/uae-iran-medical-aid-coronavirus-outbreak.html, 17 March 2020.

43 "U.S. and U.A.E. Troops Hold Major Exercise Amid Virus and Iran Tensions", https://www.nytimes.com/2020/03/23/world/middleeast/us-and-uae-troops-hold-major-exercise-amid-virus-and-iran-tensions.html, 23 March 2020.

moment.44 Logically, the world will soon see coalitions for fighting pandemic. The leading countries with advanced virology expertise will rally around to form a super-league to fight pandemics as terrorist attacks. Consolidation of the Coalition for Epidemic Preparedness Innovations45 (already launched in Davos in 2017) is likely to be the new coalition hub for the global powers.

8. *Global Bio-Defence Regime*:

The role of nuclear weapons and utility of nuclear deterrence will continue to remain at the centre-stage of global security discourse but within the prism of the new apprehension of biological warfare with the background of conspiracy theories about corona virus. While nuclear weapon states would be reluctant to discount the role of nuclear arsenal, building of a permanent bio-defence force would be a national security imperative in the post COVID-19

---

44 Peter Daszak, "We Knew Disease X Was Coming. It's Here Now",
https://www.nytimes.com/2020/02/27/opinion/coronavirus-pandemics.html, 27 February 2020.

45 CEPI, https://cepi.net/

global security discourse. The ninth review Conference of the Biological Weapons Convention is scheduled for November 2021 which may be preponed and an assessment might be undertaken by state-parties on how the COVID-19 situation evolved from the biological weapons standpoint.46 Reinforcement of the biological convention with additional verification mechanism might be pressed upon the regime or a new regime would take shape.

Besides, the post-COVID-19 world would initiate a multilateral bio-defence regime with mandatory compliance mechanism of its prescriptions on national standards on pandemic prevention policies, measures, and commitments. As pandemics respects no border, all nations have to comply with certain international standards in their preventive measures in place at the domestic level. The bilateral Indo-Pak Agreement on Reducing Risk from Accidents Relating to Nuclear Weapons model would guide putting in place such a regime at the global scale.

---

46 Tiwari, "The post COVID-19 world", https://www.orfonline.org/expert-speak/the-post-covid-19-world-63829/, 29 March 2020.

9. *The New Super Power India*:

History will remember the COVID19 outbreak as an epoch changing event that shook the global power balance. Post-pandemic, the global power hierarchy will not remain the same and the scope for redistribution of global power is unfolding. It would not be farfetched to argue that there is enough scope for nations who have relatively succeeded in fighting the pandemic and shouldered crisis responsibilities at the global level by extending valuable assistance beyond their border. India has shown the leadership quality of a Super Power of its kind especially when there is a paucity of global leadership. It amply showcased its resolve and capability to shoulder global responsibility in time of global crisis. It would be safe to vouch that India would be the fifth member of the UN Security Council (UNSC) replacing UK which has been relegated in the global power hierarchy long ago.

It is not to discount the enormity of the pandemic India is facing. Owing to huge population and inadequate medical resources at its disposal, the days ahead will be tough for India. However, India has "managed to bring its domestic requirements and global responsibilities in sync"47 during this difficult time as a responsible member of the comity of nations. When all other major powers have become inward looking while facing the pandemic, the world first time witnessed India rising beyond its immediate national concerns. All the initiatives India has shouldered "underline India's commitment to become a credible global player", says SD Muni.

When the paucity of global leadership is palpable across the world, Indian Prime Minister Narendra Modi called the SAARC conference on Covid-19 and suggested a coordinated response among the SAARC neighbours to combat coronavirus at the regional level. The video conference of SAARC leaders, where Pakistan was also on board, welcomed Modi's proposal. Modi proposed the creation of a Covid-19 emergency fund with India making an initial contribution of $10 million.48 Modi also proposed setting up of 'rapid response teams' of doctors,

---

47 Harsh V Pant, "Leadership in the time of Corona", https://www.orfonline.org/research/leadership-in-the-time-of-corona-63648/, 24 March 2020.
48 Ibid.

specialists and arrange for testing equipment, besides imparting online training to emergency response staff so as to build capacity to fight such challenges across the region. "Modi's initiative came much before any other such regional initiative and drew a positive response not only from regional states but also from countries like the US and Russia as well as the World Health Organisation."49 India's message for the world is also that it is willing and prepared, within its limited resources and capabilities, to undertake responsibilities in preserving and promoting the global common good.50

Prime Minister Modi also became the first global leader to call for a G20 summit via video conferencing to advance "a coordinated response to the COVID-19 pandemic and its human and economic implications." This was accepted by Saudi Arabia, the current chair of the G 20. In the Extraordinary Virtual G20 Leaders' Summit, Prime

---

49 Ibid.

50 SD Muni, "India has done well to revive Saarc", https://www.hindustantimes.com/analysis/india-has-done-well-to-revive-saarc-opinion/story-ax17bHXpQHzfgEPK7AaDHP.html, 16 March 2020.

Minister Modi underscored "the need to put human beings at the centre of our vision of global prosperity and cooperation, freely and openly share the benefits of medical research and development, develop adaptive, responsive and humane health care systems, promote new crisis management protocols and procedures for an interconnected global village, strengthen and reform intergovernmental organisations like WHO and work together to reduce economic hardships resulting from COVID-19 particularly for the economically weak."[51] Moreover, he called on the Leaders to help usher in a new globalization, for the collective well-being of humankind and have multilateral fora focus on promoting the shared interests of humanity.

In addition, India has undertaken tangible humanitarian measures like evacuation of nationals, supply of medical resources and support teams, above all, moral support to the needy while managing huge challenges at home. While evacuating its own

---

51 "Extraordinary Virtual G20 Leaders' Summit", https://www.narendramodi.in/the-prime-minister-narendra-modi-at-address-the-g20-virtual-summit-548983, 26 March 2020.

nationals stranded in countries like China, Iran and Italy, Manila and Singapore, India has also extended this support to nationals from Maldives, Myanmar, Bangladesh, China, US, Madagascar, Sri Lanka, Nepal, South Africa and Peru.52

Requests for emergency medical equipment from Bhutan and the Maldives have also been responded to by India. India provided 15 tonnes of medical supplies worth Rs 2.11 crore to China on 26 February53 for which China has expressed its appreciation.54 India has exported 90t of medical protective equipment to Serbia under the guidance of UNDP. Most importantly, as part of India's measures to assist neighbouring countries in dealing with the COVID-19 pandemic, "six Navy ships have been

---

52 Pant, "Leadership in the time of Corona", https://www.orfonline.org/research/leadership-in-the-time-of-corona-63648/, 24 March 2020.

53 "India provided 15 tonnes of medical supplies worth Rs 2.11 crore to coronavirus-hit China: Government", *The Economic Times*, 18 March 2020.
54 "China thanks India for offering help to battle coronavirus", https://www.indiatoday.in/world/story/china-thanks-india-offer-to-fight-coronavirus-1645100-2020-02-10, 10 February 2020.

kept ready and five medical teams are on standby by India for deployment to the Maldives, Sri Lanka, Bangladesh, Nepal, Bhutan and Afghanistan when required", the Ministry of Defence said in a statement.55

India's leadership in this time of global crisis is acknowledged and appreciated. The WHO has praised Prime Miniter Modi's initiatives to fight COVID-19 pandemic. Modi also had a telephonic conversation with US president Donald Trump. The two leaders agreed to put the full weight of the India-US partnership to fight the deadly Covid-19 disease.56 Even Modi's role and leadership is considered valuable by China when it "sought India's support to counter US bid to lay COVID-19 blame on

---

55 "Six navy ships, medical teams on standby to assist neighbouring countries",
https://www.thehindu.com/news/national/six-navy-ships-medical-teams-on-standby-to-assist-neighbouring-countries/article31249255.ece, 03 April 2020.
56"India-US partnership to fight Covid-19, says PM Modi after call with Trump",
https://www.hindustantimes.com/india-news/coronavirus-update-india-us-partnership-to-fight-covid-19-says-pm-modi-after-call-with-trump/story-wfG2IwgSu9z5Sm5jqMrOQL.html, 04 April 2020.

its door." External Affairs Minister S Jaishankar and Chinese Foreign Minister Wang Yi had a telephonic conversation prior the virtual G20 summit. Wang Yi expressed hope that "India would oppose the comments made by the US President Donald Trump and other senior officials of his administration branding the Covid-19 as a 'Chinese Virus'".57 All these and many more such remarkable leadership initiatives in the days ahead prove that India has already arrived as a forceful and reliable global power competent to shoulder global leadership.

The question logically arises where India will fit itself in the unfolding post-pandemic world order? Will it collide or cooperate with the Chinese scheme of alternative order, or supplement its new leadership power to reinvigorate the outgoing America-led world order? The notion that the USA is the only conduit to the global powerdom strongly persists in India's strategic calculations. Until now India has remained attached to, and integrating more with, the

---

57 https://www.deccanherald.com/international/world-news-politics/china-seeks-india-s-support-to-counter-us-bid-to-lay-covid-19-blame-on-its-door-817288.html

American global framework, even though Washington is still confused where to place India in its scheme. America has not been able to completely de-hyphenate India from Pakistan; it is not enthusiastic to facilitate India's entry as permanent member of the UNSC. With the strong leadership and global vision of Narendra Modi, *India must look beyond the American framework, and both compete and cooperate with China, to usher the post-pandemic world order as 'Chindian world order' to its advantage.*

Conclusion: Welcome to the New World Order

It would be highly conjectural to smear the final shape of the new world order in the offing; how soon it would emerge; and how distinct it would be from the order in vogue. Nevertheless, the COVID-19 pandemic appears to be shadowing, and simultaneously catalyzing dynamics and events that are affecting the regional and global balance in international order. In fact, wars, pandemics and large scale events accelerate redistribution of global power, hierarchy or systemic change. The pandemic has undoubtedly brought to fore the loopholes in the current global governance system, the weakness in supranational institutions, and vulnerabilities of the so-called 'developed world'.

However, no black and white answer to what the post-pandemic world order would look like; who will be on the driving seat; what would be the global power equation; whose level will be up and who will go down the hierarchy...? But certainly there will be a post-pandemic world order in which the health care paradigms, social safety nets for the most vulnerable sections of society, and crisis leadership mechanisms will have to be re-imagined and re-budgeted, because what would follow is a deep economic recession that likely to uproot the capitalist foundation on which the world is based on today.

Namaste to the post-pandemic world order whose entire *carte du jour* may not be on the table soon, but definitely in a year or two from now.

— — —

This page is intentionally left blank

NOTES: